SPOTLIGHT ON OUR FUTURE

ENERGY PROBLEMS
ON OUR EARTH

KATHY FURGANG

PowerKiDS press.

NEW YORK

Published in 2022 by The Rosen Publishing Group, Inc.
29 East 21st Street, New York, NY 10010

Copyright © 2022 by The Rosen Publishing Group, Inc.

All rights reserved. No part of this book may be reproduced in any form without permission in writing from the publisher, except by a reviewer.

First Edition

Editor: Theresa Emminizer
Book Design: Michael Flynn

Photo Credits: Cover Josemaria Toscano/Shutterstock.com; (series background) jessicahyde/Shutterstock.com; p. 4 solarseven/Shutterstock.com; p. 5 Buyenlarge/Archive Photos/Getty Images; p. 6 lusia83/Shutterstock.com; p. 7 Bettmann/Getty Images; p. 8 Vijay Talla/EyeEm/Getty Images; p. 9 Funny Solution Studio/Shutterstock.com; p. 11 U.S. Coast Guard/Getty Images; p. 12 Sunshine Seeds/Shutterstock.com; p. 13 Procyk Radek/Shutterstock.com; p. 14 Tatiana Grozetskaya/Shutterstock.com; p. 15 https://commons.wikimedia.org/wiki/File:William_Ruckelshaus_Swearing_In_as_EPA_Administrator.jpg; p. 16 https://commons.wikimedia.org/wiki/File:Donald_Trump_official_portrait.jpg; p. 17 Pacific Press/LightRocket/Getty Images; p. 18 Hulton Archive/Getty Images; p. 19 Library of Congress/Corbis Historical/Getty Images; p. 21 Bloomberg/Getty Images; p. 22 taraki/Shutterstock.com; p. 23 NASA/Getty Images; p. 25 Ververidis Vasilis/Shutterstock.com; p. 26 Noam Galai/Getty Images; p. 27 Holli/Shutterstock.com; p. 28 Jacek Chabraszewski/Shutterstock.com; p. 29 BlurryMe/Shutterstock.com.

Cataloging-in-Publication Data

Names: Furgang, Kathy.
Title: Energy problems on our Earth / Kathy Furgang.
Description: New York : PowerKids Press, 2022. | Series: Spotlight on our future | Includes glossary and index.
Identifiers: ISBN 9781725323841 (pbk.) | ISBN 9781725323872 (library bound) | ISBN 9781725323858 (6 pack)
Subjects: LCSH: Energy conservation--Juvenile literature. | Power resources--Juvenile literature.
Classification: LCC TJ163.35 F87 2022 | DDC 333.79'16--dc23

Manufactured in the United States of America

Some of the images in this book illustrate individuals who are models. The depictions do not imply actual situations or events.

CPSIA Compliance Information: Batch #CSPK22. For further information contact Rosen Publishing, New York, New York at 1-800-237-9932.

CONTENTS

WHAT IS ENERGY? 4
NONRENEWABLE RESOURCES 6
RENEWABLE RESOURCES 8
ACCIDENTS WITH ENERGY 10
A WORLD ENERGY CRISIS 12
CONSEQUENCES OF BURNING FOSSIL FUELS 14
INTERNATIONAL CLIMATE AGREEMENTS 16
UPDATING ENERGY SOLUTIONS 18
ENERGY STORAGE 20
NEW ENERGY TECHNOLOGY 22
MYTHS AND FACTS ABOUT ENERGY 24
YOUNG VOICES AND IDEAS 26
WHAT CAN YOU DO? 28
JOIN THE MOVEMENT! 30
GLOSSARY 31
INDEX 32
PRIMARY SOURCE LIST 32
WEBSITES 32

CHAPTER ONE

WHAT IS ENERGY?

Energy is the power to do something. In ancient times, people used wood as one of the first energy sources. They burned it to create heat, cook food, and keep animals away. As human populations grew bigger, they needed new sources of energy. They began using fossil fuels, such as coal, natural gas, and oil, which formed in the earth from dead plants or animals.

These wind turbines in Missouri generate, or create, electrical power. A turbine is an engine with blades that spin with pressure from water, steam, or air.

In the late 1700s, people started using new manufacturing processes. Since then, we've been burning more and more fossil fuels. This has trapped heat on Earth, increasing the temperature and harming the **environment**.

To curb the harm caused by fossil fuels, scientists began looking for better energy sources. Although people use more clean energy sources today, there's still a long way to go.

CHAPTER TWO

NONRENEWABLE RESOURCES

The Industrial Revolution was a period of economic and social growth in Europe and the United States from the late 1700s to the mid-1800s. During this time, coal became the main fuel used by industries. People burned coal to power steam engines and electric generators. Today, about 40 percent of the electricity in the world comes from coal.

In 1859, American businessman Edwin Drake drilled the first successful oil well. Oil became another main energy source. Oil is used to make other fuels, such as gasoline for cars.

Oil and coal are both nonrenewable energy sources. This means that once we use them up, there will be no more left. A renewable resource is one that can't be used up, such as wind and sunlight.

COAL

This photo shows Edwin Drake (right) standing in front of the first oil well in the United States.

CHAPTER THREE

RENEWABLE RESOURCES

In 1800, the world population was about 1 billion people. Today it's over 7 billion people. As the world population has risen, so has our energy use.

Modern societies depend on electricity. People usually generate electricity by burning fossil fuels. However, this releases **greenhouse gases**, harming the environment. We need clean, renewable energy sources more than ever.

HYDROELECTRIC DAM

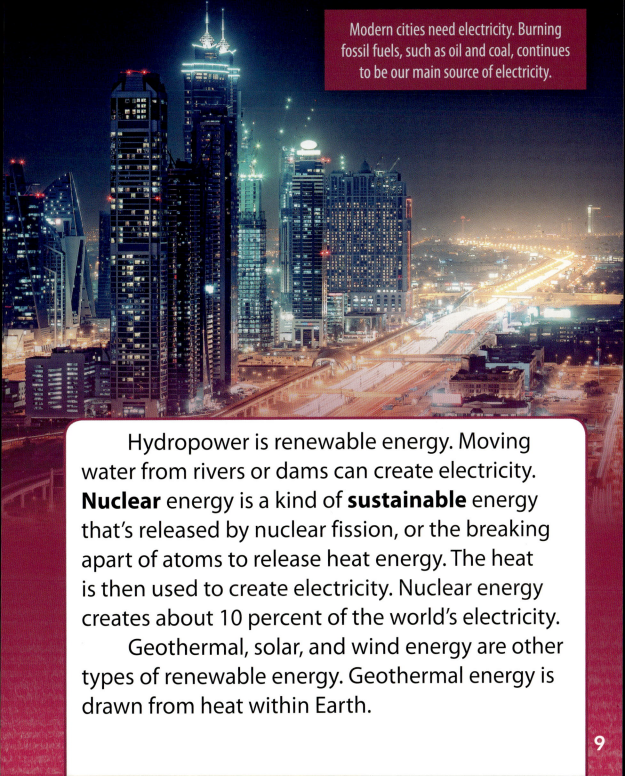

Modern cities need electricity. Burning fossil fuels, such as oil and coal, continues to be our main source of electricity.

Hydropower is renewable energy. Moving water from rivers or dams can create electricity. **Nuclear** energy is a kind of **sustainable** energy that's released by nuclear fission, or the breaking apart of atoms to release heat energy. The heat is then used to create electricity. Nuclear energy creates about 10 percent of the world's electricity.

Geothermal, solar, and wind energy are other types of renewable energy. Geothermal energy is drawn from heat within Earth.

CHAPTER FOUR

ACCIDENTS WITH ENERGY

Energy sources are helpful, but many can also cause harm. In 1986, the Soviet Union's Chernobyl nuclear power plant had a meltdown. This released a lot of **radioactive** materials into the air and land and killed 28 people right away. The nearby land became **contaminated**. The Soviet Union made the contaminated land off limits for people. It may not be safe to live there for thousands of years.

In 2010, the Deepwater Horizon oil rig in the Gulf of Mexico exploded. About 53,000 barrels of oil went into the Gulf of Mexico every day for 87 days. The oil killed tens of thousands of animals.

Blackouts happen when electricity is cut off. In 2017, there was a blackout after Hurricane Maria hit Puerto Rico. More than 100 days later, thousands of people were still without power.

The 2010 Deepwater Horizon accident in the Gulf of Mexico was the largest ocean oil spill in history. The explosion killed 11 workers and hurt 17 others.

CHAPTER FIVE

A WORLD ENERGY CRISIS

Not everyone in the world has enough energy. In 2017, about 1 billion people around the world didn't have electricity. Some places don't have the resources or systems for it. Some people live in places that are hard to reach. Other people who do have electricity don't have a steady supply of it.

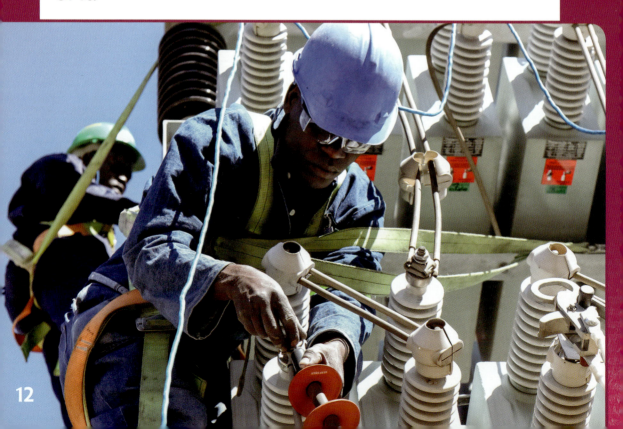

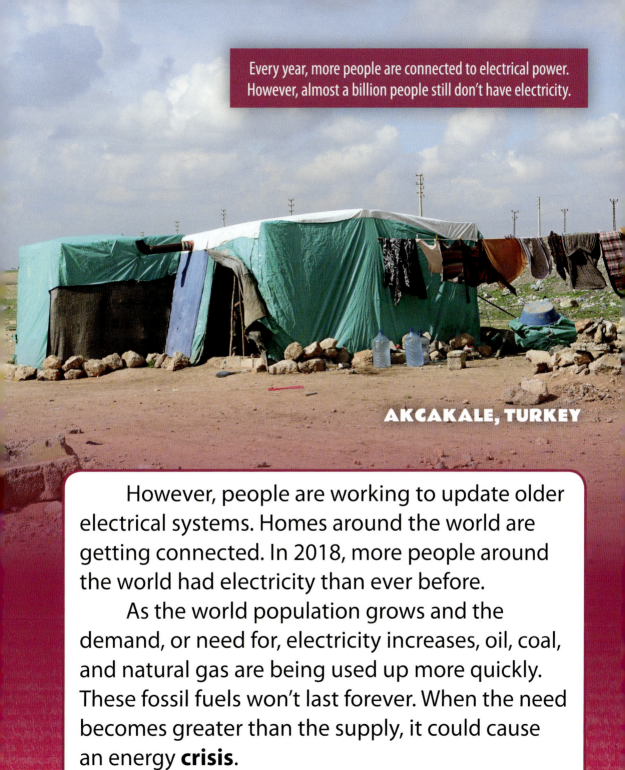

Every year, more people are connected to electrical power. However, almost a billion people still don't have electricity.

AKCAKALE, TURKEY

However, people are working to update older electrical systems. Homes around the world are getting connected. In 2018, more people around the world had electricity than ever before.

As the world population grows and the demand, or need for, electricity increases, oil, coal, and natural gas are being used up more quickly. These fossil fuels won't last forever. When the need becomes greater than the supply, it could cause an energy **crisis**.

CHAPTER SIX

CONSEQUENCES OF BURNING FOSSIL FUELS

Over the last 100 years, human activities have caused the planet to get warmer. The rising world temperature upsets the balance of natural systems. It's even pushing some species into extinction, or dying out completely.

Burning fossil fuels creates pollution that's harmful to the environment, including both animals and people. In 1952 in London, England, pollution from coal fireplaces and factories combined with foggy air. The heavy **smog** covered the city for five days, killing thousands.

William Ruckelshaus being sworn in as the first administrator, or leader, of the EPA.

Events like this drew attention to the problem of pollution. To reduce pollution and smog, many countries passed new laws that would limit **emissions** and protect the environment.

In 1963, the U.S. Congress passed the Clean Air Act. Its aim is to control the amount of harmful emissions released by factories. In 1970, the United States formed the Environmental Protection Agency (EPA).

CHAPTER SEVEN
INTERNATIONAL CLIMATE AGREEMENTS

The United Nations (UN) is an international organization that's devoted to promoting peace worldwide. In 1997, the UN recognized the need to take action about climate change caused by the use of fossil fuels. Many countries together created the Kyoto Protocol, an agreement to curb harmful greenhouse gas emissions around the world. Almost 200 countries signed it, but the United States dropped out of it in 2001.

DONALD TRUMP

On June 1, 2017, in New York City, hundreds of people voiced their concern over President Trump's decision to withdraw the United States from the Paris Climate Agreement.

In 2015, the UN agreed to increase its efforts. By 2019, 197 countries had signed the Paris Climate Agreement, which aims to keep global temperatures from rising more than 3.6°Fahrenheit (2°Celsius) over conditions before the Industrial Revolution.

However, on June 1, 2017, President Donald Trump announced the United States would withdraw from the Paris Climate Agreement. Many disagreed with this decision because the United States is one of the top producers of greenhouse gases in the world.

CHAPTER EIGHT

UPDATING ENERGY SOLUTIONS

In the late 1700s and early 1800s, means of transportation, or travel, began to change. Starting in 1855, people could buy the first gasoline-powered car.

In 1908, Henry Ford began selling his Model T automobile in the United States. By 1913, Ford's factories manufactured as many as 1,000 cars a day. As cars became more and more common, dangerous emissions grew.

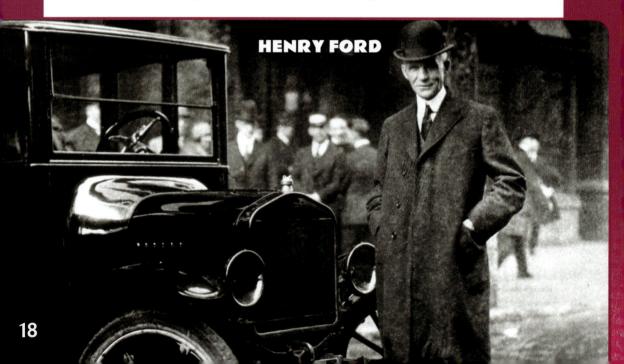
HENRY FORD

The Ford Motor Company used assembly lines to produce the Model T car. This increased the amounts manufactured and made cars cost less.

Over time, people became more concerned about this. In the 1970s, the environmental movement started. During the 1980s, people learned more about global warming. They became interested in more environmentally friendly choices.

A new hybrid electric vehicle called the Toyota Prius was released in Japan in 1997. A hybrid vehicle has a gasoline engine and an electric motor. In 2003, a group created Tesla Motors, which now sells battery-powered electric vehicles.

CHAPTER NINE
ENERGY STORAGE

When a power plant creates electricity, not all of it gets used. Some goes to waste as it's sent over electrical lines. Some gets wasted in the delivery process. Saving and storing electricity is important. This can help lower the cost of energy and reduce harmful emissions. Here are several ways to do so:

- **Large batteries can store electricity.**
- **Machines pump water into reservoirs, or man-made lakes. When more electricity is needed, the water can be released, powering turbines and generators.**
- **Unused electricity can be used to make cold water or ice. This can be used to cool systems when more power is needed.**
- **Unused kinetic energy can be stored by using large spinning machines called flywheels. Flywheels are used to power electric generators as needed.**

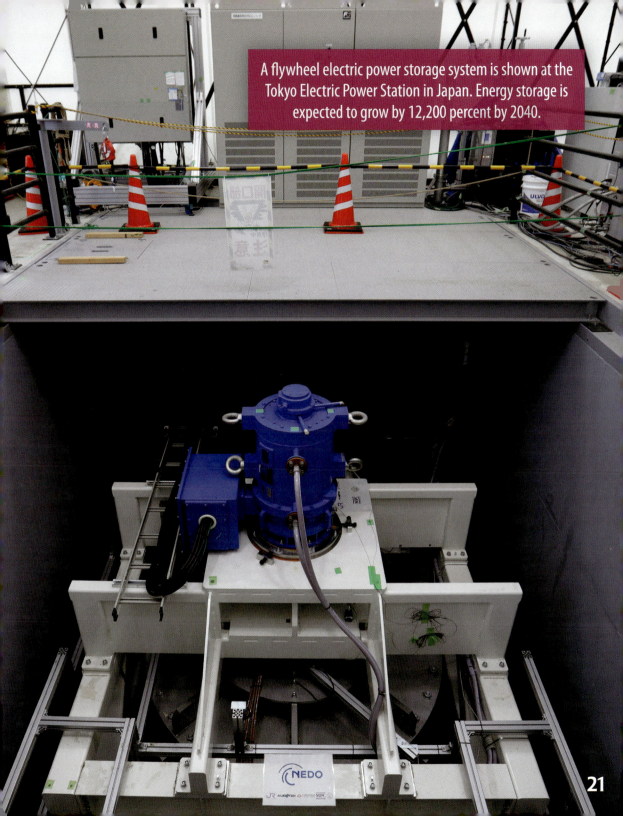

A flywheel electric power storage system is shown at the Tokyo Electric Power Station in Japan. Energy storage is expected to grow by 12,200 percent by 2040.

CHAPTER TEN

NEW ENERGY TECHNOLOGY

People are testing new renewable energy sources. Scientists are improving ways to use wind and solar energy and hydropower to make these sources more productive and cheaper.

Scientists also have new ideas about how to use **technology** to capture and create energy. Much solar energy gets lost in the atmosphere. Capturing the sun's rays in space could stop this. In 2015, scientists in Japan were able to send electric energy with microwaves, a kind of electromagnetic wave. This could allow space-based solar energy to be sent wirelessly.

The International Space Station gets some of its power from the sun. Solar panels capture the sun's rays and convert them into electricity.

Scientists from the United States and Canada have created an energy device people can wear. As a person wearing the device walks, the device may create enough electricity to power 10 mobile phones. With over 7 billion people on Earth, that's a lot of possible energy.

CHAPTER ELEVEN
MYTHS AND FACTS ABOUT ENERGY

Knowing the differences between myths and facts about energy can help people make better choices. Below are some common myths and facts about energy sources.

Myth: Solar energy is too expensive to be practical.
Fact: New solar panels are lightweight, produce more electricity, and are cheaper than older models.

Myth: Electric car batteries can't go very far before they need to be recharged.
Fact: New **lithium-ion batteries** used in electric cars store a lot of energy. Some can go as far as 370 miles (595.5 km) on a single charge.

Myth: Wind farms use more electricity than they produce.
Fact: Wind turbines create 20 to 25 times the amount of electricity that's used to build them.

A Tesla electric car recharges at a supercharger charging station. Supercharging stations help recharge cars traveling long distances.

CHAPTER TWELVE

YOUNG VOICES AND IDEAS

Young people around the world are working to help with energy and climate issues. Kallan Benson from Crownsville, Maryland, became interested in climate change when she was 9. Her environmental protests helped the state of Maryland pass a **fracking** ban.

Alexandria Villaseñor is a 14-year-old youth climate **activist**. She created an organization called Earth Uprising. The group works to convince world leaders to act now to keep the planet's warming below 3.6°Fahrenheit (2°Celsius).

ALEXANDRIA VILLASEÑOR

On March 15, 2019, students in Australia gathered to show that they want leaders to take action to address climate change.

When 15-year-old Hannah Herbst from Florida learned her friend in Ethiopia didn't have electricity, she decided to help. She invented a device that takes ocean energy and changes it into electricity. She won the top prize at the Discovery Education 3M Young Scientist Challenge in 2015.

Your voice and ideas can make a difference too!

CHAPTER THIRTEEN

WHAT CAN YOU DO?

Carbon dioxide contributes to climate change. A person's carbon footprint is how much carbon they contribute to the atmosphere. Researchers have found that typical U.S. household produces 48 tons (43.5 mt) of carbon per year. Many things may add to your carbon footprint. By making changes to reduce your carbon footprint, you are conserving energy.

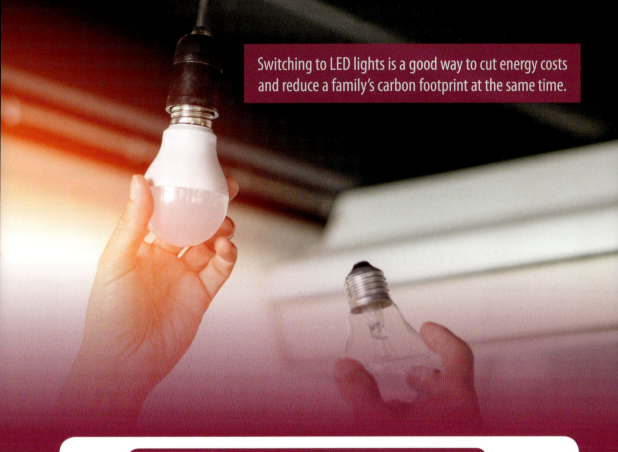

Switching to LED lights is a good way to cut energy costs and reduce a family's carbon footprint at the same time.

Here are some suggestions to reduce your carbon footprint:

- Use fewer single-use plastic items such as cups, bags, straws, and packaging material. Use reusable items instead.

- Walk or bike instead of riding in a car. If you must travel by car, then try carpooling with friends.

- Buy food that's grown locally. Local food doesn't travel as far to get to you. Foods produced in other countries require extra energy to get to you.

CHAPTER FOURTEEN
JOIN THE MOVEMENT!

A 2019 government report stated that "Earth's climate is now changing faster than at any point in the history of modern civilization primarily as a result of human activities." The good news is that new energy solutions may help us reduce fossil fuel use—and there are more new technologies on the way. Green hydrogen is hydrogen gas produced by wind and solar power. It's less harmful to the environment than hydrogen gas produced by natural gas and coal.

Everyday choices made by ordinary people help too. You can help at home by unplugging electronics that aren't being used or making other responsible decisions.

Today, young people are working hard for the environmental movement. Teen activists are using their voices to speak about climate change. Your actions and ideas could help your family, community, and the planet.

GLOSSARY

activist (AK-tih-vist) Someone who acts strongly in support of or against an issue.

contaminated (kuhn-TAA-muh-nay-tuhd) Polluted.

crisis (KRY-suhs) An unstable or difficult situation.

emission (ee-MIH-shuhn) Something that is given off, or the act of producing that thing.

environment (ihn-VY-ruhn-muht) The natural world around us.

fracking (FRA-king) A drilling technique used to extract oil and natural gas from underground.

greenhouse gas (GREEN-howz GASS) A gas in the atmosphere that traps energy from the sun.

lithium-ion battery (LIH-thee-uhm–I-ahn BA-tuh-ree) A lightweight, high-power rechargeable battery commonly used in laptops, mobile devices, and electric cars.

nuclear (NOO-klee-uhr) Used in or produced by a nuclear reaction, or one having to do with the atomic nucleus.

radioactive (ray-dee-oh-AK-tihv) Giving off rays of light, heat, or energy.

smog (SMAHG) Fog mixed with smoke.

sustainable (suh-STAY-nuh-buhl) Able to last a long time.

technology (tek-NAH-luh-jee) A method that uses science to solve problems and the tools used to solve those problems.

INDEX

B
Benson, Kallan, 26

C
Clean Air Act, 15
coal, 4, 6, 9, 13, 14, 30
Congress, U.S., 15

D
Deepwater Horizon, 10
Drake, Edwin, 6, 7

E
Earth Uprising, 26
Environmental Protection Agency (EPA), 15

F
flywheels, 20, 21
Ford, Henry, 18
fossil fuels, 4, 5, 8, 9, 13, 14, 16, 30

G
gasoline, 6, 18, 19
geothermal energy, 9
greenhouse gases, 8, 16, 17

H
Herbst, Hannah, 27
hydropower, 9, 22

K
Kyoto Protocol, 16

N
natural gas, 4, 13, 30
nuclear energy, 9

O
oil, 4, 6, 7, 9, 10, 13

P
Paris Climate Agreement, 17

S
solar energy, 9, 22, 23, 24, 30

T
Tesla Motors, 19, 25
Toyota Prius, 19
Trump, Donald, 16, 17
turbine, 5, 20, 24

U
United Nations (UN), 16, 17

V
Villaseñor, Alexandria, 26

W
water, 5, 9, 20
wind, 5, 6, 9, 22, 24, 30

PRIMARY SOURCE LIST

Page 11
Explosion at offshore drilling rig. Photograph. April 21, 2010. By U.S. Coast Guard.

Page 15
William Ruckelshaus being sworn in as the first administrator of the U.S. Environmental Protection Agency. Photograph. December 4, 1970.

Page 19
Assembly line at the Ford Motor Company's Highland Park plant. Photograph. Ca. 1913. Library of Congress.

WEBSITES

Due to the changing nature of Internet links, PowerKids Press has developed an online list of websites related to the subject of this book. This site is updated regularly. Please use this link to access the list: www.powerkidslinks.com/SOOF/energy